Little People, **BIG DREAMS**™
LEONARD COHEN

Written by
Maria Isabel Sánchez Vegara

Illustrated by
Agathe Bray-Bourret

Frances Lincoln
Children's Books

Once upon a time on the island of Montreal, Canada, there was a boy named Leonard who saw beauty where others couldn't. Whether it was a bird on a rusty wire or the stem of a rose a little too long, it was all breathtaking to him.

Every day, Leonard lost himself in the pages of his favorite comic books. And on Saturdays, at the synagogue, he listened to ancient songs and poems in wonder. The power of all these stories inspired him to find his own voice.

Sadly, his father died when he was nine. On the day of the funeral, Leonard took one of his dad's bow ties, tucked a message for him inside, and buried it in the backyard. It was the first time he had ever written something from his heart.

In high school, Leonard took photography classes,
joined the drama club, played guitar, tried cheerleading,
and even formed a folk band.

But it was when he read the poetry of a Spanish writer called Lorca that his own verses began to flow.

Things got really exciting when Leonard won a poetry competition in college. After graduating, he published his first book of poems, dedicated to his beloved father. Soon, he was the most promising young voice in Canada.

In search of inspiration, Leonard moved to Hydra,
a Greek island, where time passed slowly. There he met a
woman named Marianne, who became the muse for many of
his poems. He worked tirelessly, carefully choosing each word.

Still, it was hard to make a living as a poet, so Leonard decided to try his hand at songwriting in New York City. He settled in the Chelsea Hotel, where artists and creative souls like Andy Warhol and Janis Joplin hung out.

One day he played a song to an artist named Judy Collins, hoping she would put it on her next album. The song, "Suzanne," became one of her biggest hits. It was the beginning of a long friendship between the two.

When Judy persuaded Leonard to sing at a charity concert, everyone was moved by his heartfelt lyrics and deep voice. But he was so nervous that he walked off stage halfway through, leaving the audience longing for more.

Leonard discovered that people didn't just love his music, they also loved him! Soon after, he recorded his first album. And he continued singing for almost fifty years, writing some of the most beautiful lines the world had ever heard.

His songs were like stories told in a calm and gentle voice.
Leonard's lyrics spoke of love, war, and everything that makes
us human. And even though his melodies sounded a little
bit sad, there was always a ray of hope shining out from them.

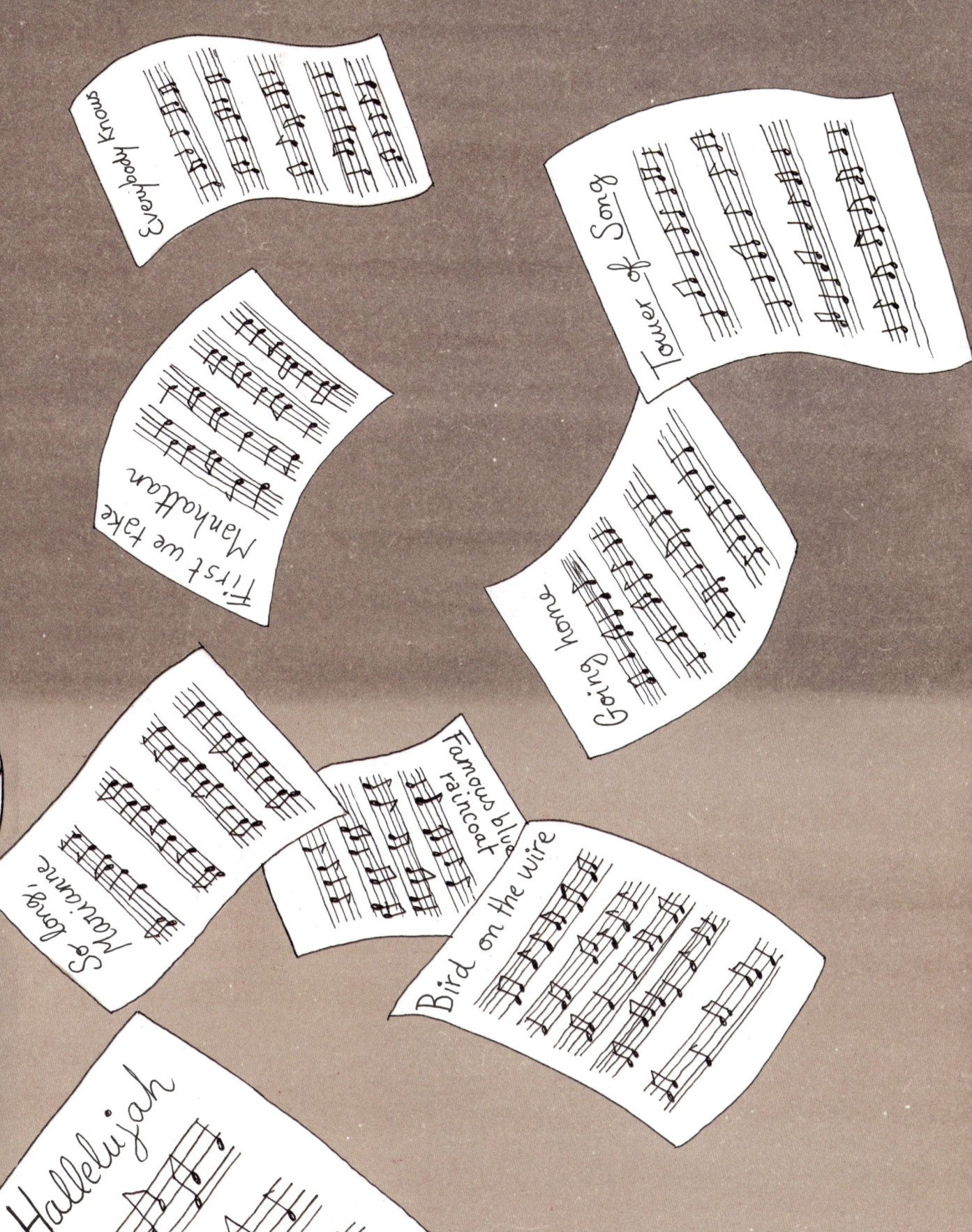

Leonard's most famous work, "Hallelujah," made him a global star, but what really mattered to him lay beyond the spotlight.

He was a loving father to Adam and Lorca and spent years in a monastery as a Zen monk.

And even now, generations of writers and musicians remember Leonard through his novels, poems, and songs. The little boy who showed the world that true beauty does not have to be perfect, it just has to move the soul.

LEONARD COHEN

(Born 1934 – Died 2016)

1967

1993

Leonard Norman Cohen grew up in Montreal, Canada, with his parents and sister, Esther. Both his grandfathers had been important figures in the city's Jewish community. Leonard felt a strong connection to his faith and attended synagogue with his family where he also learned Hebrew. As a teenager, his passion for country music inspired him to take up the guitar. At age fifteen, he fell in love with Federico García Lorca's poetry and began writing his own verses. He went on to study English literature in college, and his first book of poems was published shortly after. Supported by the Canada Council for the Arts, Leonard traveled to London, UK, but soon left for sunnier Greece. He lived on an island called Hydra and was mesmerized by the nature he saw and the people he

2008

2018

met there. Yet it was hard to make money from poetry, so, after seven years, he moved to the United States to work as a musician, using his gift for words to write songs. Leonard made friends in New York City's music scene and became known for his passionate lyrics and haunting melodies. Tunes such as "Suzanne" and "Bird on the Wire" were soon classics. But it was "Hallelujah," which took years to craft, that proved to be his biggest hit. At first his record label didn't believe in the song, but Leonard always did, and it became one of the most covered tracks in history. He released his final studio album at age eighty-two and continued writing until the end of his life. Leonard's story reminds us that all our feelings matter, and by expressing them creatively, we can connect with others and ourselves.

Want to find out more?

Have a read of this great book:

Poetry Prompts: All sorts of ways to start a poem by Joseph Coelho

With help from an adult, you can listen to Leonard Cohen's music online.

Text © 2024 Maria Isabel Sánchez Vegara. Illustrations © 2024 Agathe Bray-Bourret.
Original idea of the series by Maria Isabel Sánchez Vegara, published by Alba Editorial, s.l.u.
"Little People, BIG DREAMS" and "Pequeña & Grande" are trademarks of
Alba Editorial s.l.u. and/or Beautifool Couple S.L.
First Published in the USA in 2024 by Frances Lincoln Children's Books, an imprint of The Quarto Group.
100 Cummings Centre, Suite 265D, Beverly, MA 01915, USA. T +1 978-282-95900 www.Quarto.com
All rights reserved.

No part of this publication may be reproduced, stored in a retrieval system, or transmitted, in any form,
or by any means, electrical, mechanical, photocopying, recording, or otherwise without the prior written
permission of the publisher or a license permitting restricted copying.

This book is not authorized, licensed, or approved by the estate of Leonard Cohen.
Any faults are the publisher's who will be happy to rectify for future printings.
A CIP record for this book is available from the Library of Congress.
ISBN 978-0-7112-9473-8
Set in Futura BT.

Published by Peter Marley · Designed by Sasha Moxon
Commissioned by Lucy Menzies · Edited by Molly Mead
Production by Nikki Ingram
Grateful thanks to Hannah Srour-Zackon for her consultation.

Manufactured in Shanghai, China CC052024
1 3 5 7 9 8 6 4 2

Photographic acknowledgments (pages 28-29, from left to right): 1. Portrait of Canadian poet, novelist, and musician Leonard Cohen
(1934 - 2016), dressed in black, as he writes in a notebook, August 1967 © Jack Robinson via Getty Images. 2. Leonard Cohen
performing at the Paramount Theater in New York City on June 14, 1993 © Ebet Roberts/Redferns via Getty Images. 3. Leonard
Cohen The Glastonbury Festival - Day 3 Glastonbury, England - 29.06.08 © WENN Rights Ltd via Alamy Stock Photo. 4. Photo taken
in March 2018 shows a mural of late Canadian poet, novelist and singer-songwriter, Leonard Cohen, drawn in the heart of his
hometown Montreal in time for the anniversary of his death © Kyodo News Stills via Getty Images.

MIX
Paper | Supporting
responsible forestry
FSC® C008047
FSC
www.fsc.org

Collect the Little People, BIG DREAMS™ series:

FRIDA KAHLO	COCO CHANEL	MAYA ANGELOU	AMELIA EARHART	AGATHA CHRISTIE	MARIE CURIE	ROSA PARKS	AUDREY HEPBURN	EMMELINE PANKHURST

ELLA FITZGERALD	ADA LOVELACE	JANE AUSTEN	GEORGIA O'KEEFFE	HARRIET TUBMAN	ANNE FRANK	MOTHER TERESA	JOSEPHINE BAKER	L. M. MONTGOMERY

JANE GOODALL	SIMONE DE BEAUVOIR	MUHAMMAD ALI	STEPHEN HAWKING	MARIA MONTESSORI	VIVIENNE WESTWOOD	MAHATMA GANDHI	DAVID BOWIE	WILMA RUDOLPH

 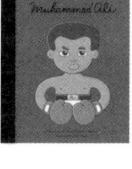   

DOLLY PARTON	BRUCE LEE	RUDOLF NUREYEV	ZAHA HADID	MARY SHELLEY	MARTIN LUTHER KING JR.	DAVID ATTENBOROUGH	ASTRID LINDGREN	EVONNE GOOLAGONG

BOB DYLAN	ALAN TURING	BILLIE JEAN KING	GRETA THUNBERG	JESSE OWENS	JEAN-MICHEL BASQUIAT	ARETHA FRANKLIN	CORAZON AQUINO	PELÉ

ERNEST SHACKLETON	STEVE JOBS	AYRTON SENNA	LOUISE BOURGEOIS	ELTON JOHN	JOHN LENNON	PRINCE	CHARLES DARWIN	CAPTAIN TOM MOORE

HANS CHRISTIAN ANDERSEN	STEVIE WONDER	MEGAN RAPINOE	MARY ANNING	MALALA YOUSAFZAI	ANDY WARHOL	RUPAUL	MICHELLE OBAMA	MINDY KALING

IRIS APFEL · ROSALIND FRANKLIN · RUTH BADER GINSBURG · MARILYN MONROE · KAMALA HARRIS · ALBERT EINSTEIN · CHARLES DICKENS · YOKO ONO · MICHAEL JORDAN

NELSON MANDELA · PABLO PICASSO · AMANDA GORMAN · GLORIA STEINEM · FLORENCE NIGHTINGALE · HARRY HOUDINI · J.R.R. TOLKIEN · ELVIS PRESLEY · NEIL ARMSTRONG

ALEXANDER VON HUMBOLDT · NIKOLA TESLA · WILMA MANKILLER · MARCUS RASHFORD · LAVERNE COX · MAE JEMISON · DWAYNE JOHNSON · HELEN KELLER · ANNA PAVLOVA

QUEEN ELIZABETH · TERRY FOX · HEDY LAMARR · SHAKIRA · FREDDIE MERCURY · LEWIS HAMILTON · LOUIS PASTEUR · PRINCESS DIANA · DAVID HOCKNEY

VANESSA NAKATE · OLIVE MORRIS · KING CHARLES · MOZART · STEVE IRWIN · JÜRGEN KLOPP · LEO MESSI · SALLY RIDE · TENZING NORGAY

KYLIE MINOGUE · BEYONCÉ · TAYLOR SWIFT · RAFA NADAL · USAIN BOLT · SIMONE BILES

STAN LEE · LEONARD COHEN

Scan the QR code for free activity sheets, teachers' notes and more information about the series at www.littlepeoplebigdreams.com